Holy Island of Lindi

Steve Newman & Catherine Sanderson Photography by Graeme Peacock

Holy Island of Lindisfarne

There aren't that many places where you can step out of the car, take in 2,000 years of history and at the same time soak up views of breathtaking beauty that constantly change throughout the seasons. Holy Island, or Lindisfarne as it is also known, lying five miles off the A1 on the Northumberland coast, is definitely one of these places. However, the last two miles of the approach are across a causeway, which is flooded by the tide twice a day for five hours at a time.

There is a large car park as you drive onto the island and one for disabled drivers further inland. Holy Island can be swamped with visitors at peak times so if possible plan your visit for the quieter periods. Please don't park in the village as this causes tremendous congestion in the narrow streets and results in the disruption of deliveries to the homes and businesses of the islanders.

If you have dogs with you, please make sure they are not running in an area where the pirri-pirri bur is growing as this can spoil your visit to the island. The plant is not native to the island but comes from New Zealand; it probably arrived on the island by being washed down the river Tweed from the fleeces being prepared in the Scottish woollen mills. It has very tight sticky burrs that can coagulate in a huge mass in a dog's fur resulting, sometimes, in the fur needing to be trimmed down to the skin to remove it. Natural England does a wonderful job in controlling and trying to eradicate the burr but be warned, it is better to be safe than sorry!

Clockwise from top left: St Cuthbert's Island / Crossing over to Lindisfarne / Warnings about Pirri-Pirri! / Oystercatcher

The Causeway

The Island is accessed by road from the mainland over the causeway that runs across the sands and alongside the dunes until it reaches Chare Ends. A second causeway follows a line of poles, erected in 1860, directly across the sand and this has been used since the earliest times. This crossing is still used today by long distance walkers, pilgrims and those who wish to experience crossing the tidal flats.

If walking across do plan, for safety's sake, to arrive about an hour before the end of the safe crossing time for the road because depending on the direction and strength of the wind the tide may well come in quicker than normal.

The arrival of the motorcar resulted in the new causeway being built in 1954, extended in 1965, and rebuilt and raised in 2004. Visitors who have ignored the safe crossing times and are caught by the incoming tide regularly use the rescue boxes you see on the sand flats and on the bridge over the South Low Channel. It is not unknown for an RAF helicopter to come and rescue families sitting on top of their cars.

Tide tables can be found at the ends of the causeway, in the car parks, in the village square and at the Beal crossroads on the A1. You will also find them in the *Berwick Advertiser, Northumberland Gazette* and on the island's website.

Pilgrims crossing over the tidal flats to Lindisfarne

3

The island is not quite cut off from civilisation at high tide as much as you might think. In the case of fire an RAF helicopter from nearby Boulmer would bring in a fire crew from the mainland to use the island's fire engine which is stored in the building on the corner of Chare Ends and Green Lane. The fire station plaque can still be seen on the wall. In a medical emergency the air ambulance or an RAF helicopter comes and collects the patient and delivers them to the relevant hospital on the mainland depending on the nature of the emergency.

Whilst crossing the causeway look out for redshank feeding by the side of the road, longtailed ducks sitting in the channel under the bridge and eider ducks, known locally as Cuddy Ducks as they were St. Cuthbert's favourite bird.

As you come onto the island during the summer look out for the Maize Maze. Open from July this five acre site has over a mile of pathways for all the family to get lost in! In winter, it is left standing as shelter and food for the Island's bird life. There are also fresh fruit and vegetables grown on the island available just down the road from the car park.

The Snook and North Shore

A road turning off the causeway road about a mile after you come onto the island reaches the Snook and the North Shore. This road can be very seriously potholed so do take care when you drive along it. At the end, you will find a small car park and an information board. You will see the Snook to the west whilst a short walk eastwards will bring you onto the beach of the North Shore.

It is thought that the Snook was once separate from the island; nowadays it is connected by the sandy neck you drive along to reach the village. To the east of this is an area now called the Links and you can walk back to Chare Ends, where the causeway road comes onto the island, along the old western Waggonway.

The high tower at the Snook is something of a mystery and it is thought that it could have been the winding tower of a coalmine that operated here in the eighteenth century, but there is no sign of winding gear inside or indeed the shaft itself. At one point the tower was described as a flag signalling station but the fact remains exactly why this elaborate little tower is standing here is still a mystery.

A walk eastwards along the North Shore beach will bring you to Snipe Point with a natural arch and some caves. The small bay here is known as Coves Haven.

Top Left: Redshank / Top Right: The Snook / Above: The refuge post on the causeway

The Village

Walk along Chare Ends from the main car park into the village, past the Lindisfarne Hotel on the corner of Green Lane. If you turn left here, you will see St. Aidan's Catholic Church, and at the end of the road there is a car park for the disabled and public toilets.

The Lindisfarne Hotel offers refreshments and lunches and on your right you'll notice the old fire station still with the volunteer plaque fixed to the wall. The fire station was closed in the early 1990s and the island now relies on an RAF helicopter to help in an emergency.

Walking down towards the main street of the village you will see the Island Oasis Café which serves snacks and lunches. A little further along, next to Celtic Crafts, is the Pilgrims Coffee House with its lovely walled garden, ideal for al fresco coffee breaks. Inside there is a welcoming atmosphere with more seating in the cosy rooms upstairs.

On your left is Front Street, which will take you up to the castle and to the right is Marygate that leads to the Lindisfarne Centre, the Gospel Garden and the Post Office. You will see a signpost on the other side of the road directing you to the island's places of interest. Directly opposite you is Crossgates Lane in which you'll find a public phone box, the site of the old village hall and another set of public toilets before entering into the Market Place.

In the Market Place is the Celtic Cross designed by John Dobson, the great architect who transformed Newcastle and Northumberland in the nineteenth century. Set up in 1828, it is situated where the original Market Cross stood and stands on the pedestal of an earlier cross. The original stump was taken to a place near the parish church where it is still used as a Petting Stone, which every island bride jumps over for luck.

The Celtic Cross in the Market Place (Photo: Brian Young)

On 14th August 1931, Edward de Stein, owner of the castle, generously provided Holy Island with a village hall. In recent years the hall has fallen into disrepair and has now been demolished. However there is an active campaign to raise money to build a new village hall. In 1944, Sir Edward presented the castle to the National Trust and he remained there as a tenant until he died in 1965.

Around the Market Place

The picturesque cottage below, situated in the Market Place, is one of the oldest on the island and is now a private house. It has been in the same family for generations and for many years was the village post office. As the postmaster travelled to the mainland to collect the post, he used one end of the cottage as a stable for his horse.

Various routes lead off from the Market Place. To the west, you'll see the St. Aidan's Winery and the St. Cuthbert's Centre. To the south the path leads to the Priory, the Visitors Centre and the Parish Church of St. Mary the Virgin. The south-east corner, by the side of the Crown and Anchor will take you across the meadow to the Heugh, whilst the north-east corner will take you into Fenkle Street where you can rejoin Front Street or turn right into St. Cuthbert's Square and come out further down on the road to the castle. The square is also one of the pickup points for the minibus shuttle that runs between the castle and the car park.

As part of their diet the monks produced mead from honey, a popular drink in the middle ages. Couples would drink it for a month after their wedding to ensure fertility, a fact that may have given us our word 'honeymoon'. The brew house can still be seen in the Priory and St. Aidan's Winery on the island still carries on the tradition of making mead today. The firm also continues the monks' reputation for hospitality by offering visitors a free sample of Lindisfarne Mead, the only mead made on the island. It is a unique alcoholic fortified wine manufactured here on the island from fermented white grapes, honey, herbs, pure natural water from the island's artesian well and fortified with fine spirits.

Lindisfarne village

The Gospel Garden

The Gospel Garden is to be found in Marygate, just to the east of the Post Office and opposite the Lindisfarne Centre and is a floral vision of one of this country's greatest cultural treasures. The garden lies only yards away from where the Lindisfarne Gospels were created and the Lindisfarne Centre now houses an interactive display where you can gain more information.

This garden was created by Mr Stan Timmins and his son Liam and it won a silver award at the 2003 Chelsea Flower Show. The garden was given to the island as a gift after the show and arrived at its final destination with the help of the Holy Island of Lindisfarne Community Trust that acquired an allotment from Lady Rose Crossman. Funding was secured from Northumberland Strategic Partnership and the Local Heritage Initiative. The Gospel Garden sets out to represent the colourful imagery and religious strengths of the original Gospels.

The intricate lettering of the Gospels is represented by circular flowerbeds and rockeries. The entrance features a large Celtic cross representing heaven and earth. On each of the four faces lettering in Latin proclaims *'IN HOC SINGULARI SIGN VITA REDDITUR MUNDO' - In this unique sign life is restored to the world.* This wording has been taken from the ancient stone cross in St. Paul's Monastery in Jarrow where the Venerable Bede lived for most of his life, visiting Lindisfarne only once. Bede was a great scholar who wrote, amongst many other books, 'The Ecclesiastical History of the English Nation'. If you have time to take a trip south of the river Tyne, a visit to the remains of the monastery and Bede's World at the Museum of Early Medieval Northumbria at Jarrow is certainly worthwhile.

The garden also features a large sculpture by Fenwick Lawson called the 'Fragmented Cross', which represents the stages of the journey the monks made with St. Cuthbert's body over many years before he was laid to rest at Durham. At the rear of the garden is a decorative panel representing a reredos, a free-standing decorated screen, usually found behind an altar. This is visible through an arch, which represents the famous rainbow arch of the Priory. Beneath the arch, the ground is covered in glass particles, which sparkle in the sunlight in various shades of blue mingled with white.

The Gospel Garden

The oldest inhabited Elizabethan house in the village was built in 1568 and is now occupied by the Community of Aidan and Hilda and called The Open Gate Retreat House. This is the main house of this Community, which is a scattered community of Christians of all denominations who draw inspiration from the Celtic saints.
They run an extensive programme of retreats and study weeks. Inside the main entrance is a specialist bookshop and through a door in the courtyard, if you go down the old stone stairs to the basement, you come across an unusual little chapel where on weekdays prayers are held at midday and 9pm.

St. Cuthbert's Centre

A small wrought-iron gate takes you into a peaceful garden with some welcoming benches, one of them marking the Centre as the beginning and end of St. Cuthbert's Way, a popular walk from Melrose to Holy Island. Sitting on the benches and looking to the left of the gate, you can see a small sculpture with a tiny staircase. This is just one of the intriguing sculptures that you will see as you walk round the Centre garden. Look out for, amongst others, Simon, a reclining figure gazing skywards who was modelled on an unsuspecting passer-by while Jean Parker was sculpting in the garden. If you walk round to what was the old entrance to the church you will see Jean's sculpture *The Cross* and its companion piece *Mary at the Foot of the Cross*. These wonderful sculptures were created between 1999 and 2001. There is also a 'font' bird bath and you may be lucky enough to see some birds enjoying it.

At the right hand side of the Centre a path leads you to the Old Boiler House Chapel and when you open the door on a sunny day it seems pitch black until your eyes get used to the change of light. This tiny chapel has a special atmosphere all of its own and it is open every day throughout the year. It is a simple site of honest labour where the fire was set so that the congregation, mostly fishermen and their families, in the church could be warm whilst worshipping.

Entering the St. Cuthbert's Centre through the porch, you come into a light, airy and comfortable multipurpose hall which can be a sanctuary, a workshop or a place to share food. The Centre is open to the public from morning prayer at 9.15 a.m. until dusk when it is not booked by groups using it for Quiet Days or Retreats. Small groups visiting the island may be able to book a reflective prayer

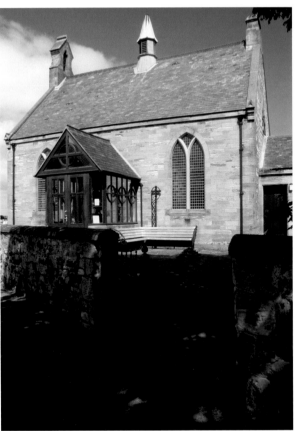

The St. Cuthbert's Centre

walk around Holy Island by contacting the director in advance of their visit. Upstairs there is an interesting display on the history of the Centre. It all started on a Saturday evening in December 1832 when the first Presbyterian minister to serve on Holy Island, Alexander Moody, travelled across the sands in a high-wheeled mail cart. He served here until 1835 and was much loved by the Islanders, especially for his tireless work in the cholera epidemic of 1834. This new church was opened in 1892 by the Rev. Robert Stewart and it seated 200 people and cost £200 to build. It became part of the United Reformed Church in 1972 but by 1990, like many churches, the congregation faced closure or a new vision of ministry and mission. The St. Cuthbert's Centre is the magnificent result of this new vision and it is a National Mission Project of the United Reformed Church. Everyone is welcome to visit the Centre.

Some of the intriguing sculptures in the garden of the St, Cuthbert's Centre

St. Cuthbert's Isle

Lying just off the southwest corner of the island below the church is St. Cuthbert's Isle. It got its name as St. Cuthbert used it as a hermitage and the cross you can see marks the spot of the altar. Before its present name it was know as Thrush Isle or Hob Thrush. It is well worth a walk out to here at low tide as you can get superb views of the flats and the causeway; however these rocks can be very slippery, so do take care on the way. Take a pair of binoculars with you and you should get some good views of the seals basking on the flats.

On the beach opposite, you may find, if you're lucky, small lead-coloured discs called St Cuthbert's Beads. In fact, they are the fossilised remains of ancient sea creatures called *crinoids* or *stone lilies* and *feather stars*. They are millions of years old and are related to our modern sea urchins.

Looking back on to the island, the cliffs you can see are made of boulder clay that was deposited here during the last Ice Age. To the south of these cliffs is a small barn-like building with a pale green double door. This is the old lifeboat station and on either side of the door are two plaques. Interestingly enough their age is revealed by the fact that the inscription reads R.N.L.B.I. as opposed to the modern RNLI

There was another lifeboat station on the island and the remains of the slipway where the boat was launched can be made out beneath the modern look-out tower on the Heugh at very low tides.

St. Cuthbert's Isle

St. Aidan and St. Cuthbert

St Aidan

The statue you see just to the north of the priory is that of St. Aidan. He is carrying the torch of the gospel to light up the world and it was he who set up a monastery here in AD 635 at the invitation of King Oswald of Northumbria, who lived in the fortress of Bamburgh just across the bay.

St. Aidan was a Celtic monk, probably born in Ireland about AD 600 who lived for many years on the Island of Iona, off the west coast of Scotland. He was consecrated as a Bishop and sent to Northumbria in AD 634. By choosing Lindisfarne as his monastic centre, his monks could have some seclusion when the island was cut off from the mainland but they could easily walk across the sands at low tide to the mainland or to the King's house at Bamburgh. None of the original buildings from the first monastery have survived, as they were most probably made of wood and sited on the Heugh or where the stone ruins of the later Benedictine Priory now lie.

St. Aidan and his monks lived sparingly and dressed in rough clothes of wool and leather and although St. Aidan is often depicted in the robes of a Franciscan friar he lived long before St. Francis and before the Benedictines came to England.

Although often overshadowed by St. Cuthbert, Aidan's contribution to the development of Christianity in Britain is immense. With just twelve monks, he set up an institution from which, over time, missionaries spread out founding abbeys and monasteries across the land. He died at Bamburgh in AD 651.

Inside the priory is a bronze statue of St. Cuthbert. On the night St. Aidan died Cuthbert was tending sheep and received a vision that prompted him to join the monastery at Melrose. He eventually sought solitude on the Farne Islands, becoming Bishop of Lindisfarne in AD 685. During his time as bishop, he travelled hundreds of miles on foot and on horseback searching for those who had not heard the Gospel to try to bring them to the faith. In AD 687, he resigned as bishop, as he felt very ill, and went back to Inner Farne where he died. His body was brought back to Lindisfarne and buried in the little church of St. Peter on 20th March, AD 687.

St. Aidan walked everywhere so that he could meet and talk to people. The King wanted to help St. Aidan so he presented him with a horse, but St. Aidan gave it away to a beggar.

St. Aidan gave women a chance to form their own monastic life under the guidance of St. Hilda, who was the first great Abbess, ruling houses at Hartlepool and Whitby.

The Viking raids forced the monks to flee in AD 875, taking the body of St. Cuthbert with them, finally ending up at Durham in 1070. where the body still remains. The monks had always intended to return to Lindisfarne with the coffin but were waiting for the Vikings to stop raiding the coast of England. When this happened they set off to make their way back. This is only one of the many different versions of this story:

As the monks were carrying the coffin it became very heavy and they had not the strength to move it. They thought that St. Cuthbert was trying to tell them something so they waited and one of the monks had a vision of St. Cuthbert who said he wanted to be buried at Dunholme. The monks were perplexed as they had no idea where this was, but then they heard two peasant women calling to each other. One said, 'I've lost my cow.' The other replied, 'I've seen your cow on Dunholme'. The monks persuaded the women to show them the way and this time the coffin was light and easy to move. They found the cow and there they laid the body of the saint and built over it the first Durham Cathedral, made of branches and straw.

In time the temporary shrine was replaced by a better wooden one, then by a stone church and eventually by the magnificent Norman cathedral we see today. Next time you go to Durham Cathedral look quite high up on the outside next to Dun Cow Lane and you will see a carving of the cow and the women. The tomb of St Cuthbert is behind the high altar.

The monks returned to the island in 1082 to form the Benedictine Priory in memory of St. Cuthbert. Today long distance walkers complete the 62 - mile St. Cuthbert's Way walk from Melrose to the island, finishing by crossing the bay at low tide.

Sculpture of St. Cuthbert by Fenwick Lawson

St. Cuthbert returned home to visit his foster mother and found the whole village in a panic as a fire had just started in one of the houses, threatening to spread through the whole village.
He said, "Do not worry, mother. You and yours will be safe, no matter how fierce the flame". He lay down, full length on the ground outside the house and prayed and suddenly the wind changed and his mother's house and the village were saved.

The Parish Church of St. Mary the Virgin

The Parish Church of St. Mary the Virgin

From the outside, the nineteenth century bell tower dominates the church, whilst the southern wall has amazing patterns where the wind and rain have eroded the weaker parts of the stones. Just outside the eastern end of the church is the huge socket of St. Cuthbert's Cross that stood in the village green. Now it is called the Petting Stone and brides, assisted by two of the oldest fishermen, jump over it to ensure a happy marriage.

The Parish Church of St. Mary the Virgin was long the mother church of the district of Islandshire, which covered a large area of the mainland. As you walk into the church, the oldest building on the island, on your left is a stained glass window of St. Aidan commemorating Edward de Stein, knight 1887 - 1965 and Miss Gladys de Stein 1891 - 1968. The family were the previous owners of the castle.

The south aisle, built in 1304, has interesting displays showing the seventh century structure that stood here. There is also a fascinating and very atmospheric,

wooden carving representing the monks carrying St. Cuthbert's body on their journey to Durham by the sculptor Fenwick Lawson. A display case contains replicas of the Lindisfarne Gospels and the Book of Kells.

The north aisle is immediately recognisable as Norman by its sweeping arches, including the famous 'Leaning Pillar of Lindisfarne'; the alternating of red and white stone is the only example to be found in Northumberland. Above the chancel arch some original Saxon work can still be seen. On the north wall of the sanctuary is the oldest memorial in the church, thought to be from the twelfth century and appears to depict a mitre and a cross with a sword. There is a splendid reredos in the sanctuary, which shows the Saints, Aidan, Cuthbert, Bede, Oswald, Columba and Wilfrid as well as the Blessed Virgin Mary and St. John at the foot of the Cross. At the back of the church, there are for sale some very interesting leaflets about the history of the church and the lives of some of these saints.

The design of the Fishermen's altar carpet is taken from the St. Luke's 'carpet page' of the Lindisfarne Gospels. This carpet was made by the Island women from a design by Jean Freer from Castleton in North Yorkshire.

The Benedictine monks probably used this church until the Priory church was completed.

St. Mary's is the only building on the island with any Saxon work visible within it.

A story told by Reginald of Durham in the late twelfth century describes a miraculous appearance of Cuthbert and his followers coming out of the parish church and entering the Priory by the west door, celebrating mass in the Priory and then returning to St. Mary's.

Above: Stained glass window, picturing St. Aidan and commemorating the de Stein family

Left: The monks carrying St. Cuthbert's body. 'The Journey' by Fenwick Lawson A.R.C.A.

On the floor of the high altar is a beautiful carpet in the design of the St. Mark 'carpet page' of the Lindisfarne Gospels that were written here in the Golden Age of Celtic Christianity. Miss Kathleen Parbury had the idea for this carpet and brought it to fruition with the help of students from Alnwick College of Education who transferred the design onto canvas and eighteen women from Holy Island who then made the carpet.

St. Mary's is a very welcoming church and has at least three services every day of the year.

Outside, beside the west wall of the churchyard, on the lane leading down to the old lifeboat station, you will find the Monastic Garden. This strip of garden on either side of the gate abounds with cottage flowers for decorating the church to the north and native species deliberately planted to encourage wildlife to the south. The flowers used for decorating the church include red and white flowering currant and plants with variegated foliage. Amongst the cottage plants are some that are particularly associated with St. Mary such as marigold, lady's mantle and rosemary.

The Fishermen's altar carpet in St Mary's Church

The colour blue was used by medieval artists to paint the Madonna's robes and so this colour dominates both the cottage and wildlife sections with plants such as cornflower, vipers bugloss and wild geranium. Towards the sea, near the high tomb in the west churchyard wall, only low growing plants such as knapweed to encourage butterflies can stand up to the salt and the south-westerly wind.

The Monastic Garden

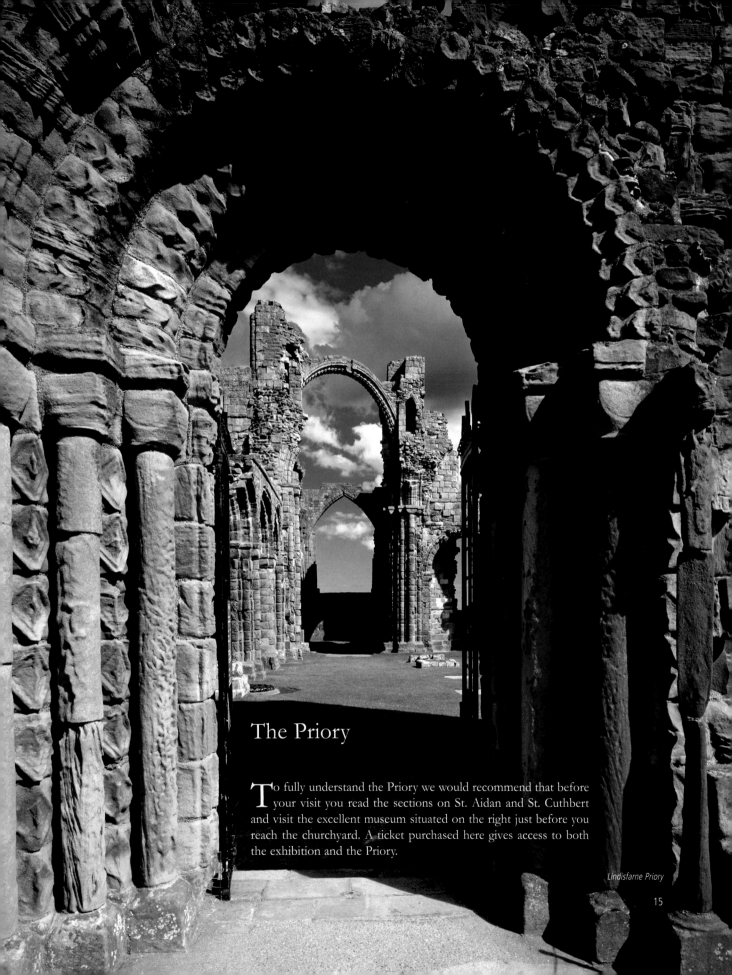

The Priory

To fully understand the Priory we would recommend that before your visit you read the sections on St. Aidan and St. Cuthbert and visit the excellent museum situated on the right just before you reach the churchyard. A ticket purchased here gives access to both the exhibition and the Priory.

Lindisfarne Priory

The priory buildings we see today were not constructed until the twelfth century, and other buildings were added a hundred years later. The rich red sandstone came from across the bay but time, wind and rain have caused it to lose some of its colour and grandeur.

Lindisfarne Priory

The original Celtic monastery would have been constructed of wattle-and-daub huts with stonework taking over as the years progressed. The exact location of the Celtic buildings is not known but as both the Parish Church of St Mary and the ruined Priory Church next to it are in a straight line on an east-west alignment it is possible that the area between the two may well have been the pivotal point of the monastery.

You enter the church of the Priory by the west door with its ornate Norman carving above. Straight away, you can see what made Lindisfarne Priory so unusual in the Middle Ages as still visible are two cross-shaped arrow loops inserted for protection against raids by the Scots. There were once two turrets either side of the doorway but now only one remains on the south side reaching almost to its original height.

On entering the nave of the church, you will notice the famous rainbow arch in front of you. This is one of the ribs that supported the central tower of the church and it has some intricate carved chevron markings on it. Similar fascinating carvings can be found on the piers of the nave, remarkably like those at Durham Cathedral. The entire church was vaulted in stone, showing the importance of Lindisfarne, as this was a highly unusual feature in English churches.

Standing under the rainbow arch you have the small north and south transepts either side of you, each having a shallow circular apse on the east side that probably held a side altar. A spiral staircase on the west end of each apse led up to galleries above and these can still be seen. To the east of the rainbow arch is the chancel, which was extended in the twelfth century. This involved the demolishing of the original curved apse, the foundations of which are still visible. The chancel was where the main altar of the church was situated, the three large windows date from the fourteenth century and originally would have been much grander with stone tracery.

Unlike the church, the monastic buildings are built of grey stone and date from a later period. You access them by walking through a doorway from the south transept into what was the sacristy where the relics belonging to the church were housed. This then blends into the Chapter House where the brothers would have met to discuss Priory business and above here was their dormitory. To the south of the Chapter House is the Parlour and the Warming Room with its large chimney block and fireplaces. The monks would have come here to keep warm and the stairs to the Prior's main room above can still be seen. To the west of the Warming House was the Refectory where the monks ate their meals and where you can still see the square open hearth in the floor.

Lindisfarne Priory

If you stand in the Refectory and look northwards, you will be able to make out what remains of the Cloisters that were intended for contemplation and study. Walking westwards, take a left turn, pass through the remains of a porch, and walk between two low walls leading out into the outer court. These are all that remains of the defensive gateway known as a barbican, which commanded the entrance to the Priory, an intact version can be seen at Alnwick Castle.

Walking through the barbican, you come into the outer court where visitors to the Priory would have entered via the main gate in the north-west corner of the wall. To all intents and purposes, this area would have resembled a bustling farmyard and the visitors would cross the court to the guest-house accommodation in the opposite corner.

Against the south wall, running east to west, are a series of buildings. The first may have been a stable, next is a room that contains a kiln, another has a well and in the south-west corner is one that has the remains of a vat. If you look carefully at the west wall, you will see the remains of a walkway for sentries with battlements and the site of the main gatehouse in the north-west corner of the court.

Here you will see Fenwick Lawson's bronze sculpture 'Cuthbert of Farne'. The original version was made of elm and you would be forgiven at first glance for thinking this was made of the same material and then painted this turquoise colour. Walk back through the barbican and turn left into the kitchen and the larder, which has a pit in the floor that was once lined with lead to keep food cool. Beyond are two rooms added in the fourteenth century, one has a brick lined circular oven and was probably the bakehouse, next is the brew-house with a sink or mash tub let into the floor.

Moving northwards, along the west wall of the cloisters you can see the remains of three vaulted rooms and these were probably used as a pantry and cellars for butter, wine and utensils. You can now return to your starting point but if you look ahead in the north wall, you will see the blocked-up doorway of what was the usual entrance to the church. The west entrance by which we entered was originally used only for ceremonial purposes.

Lindisfarne Priory

The Lindisfarne Centre

Above and below: Exhibits at The Heritage Centre

The Lindisfarne Centre in Marygate is run by the Island Community Trust and visitors to Holy Island will find there a wealth of useful information on gift shops, bed and breakfast establishments, hotels, churches and places to eat. Forthcoming activities are displayed on the village notice board. There is internet access, a lovely gift shop, accessible toilets and baby comfort facilities.

The Centre has an exhibition of the Lindisfarne Gospels where you can turn the pages of this most beautiful of manuscripts in a virtual copy housed in the Centre's computer. The interactive touch-screen programme faithfully reproduces the vibrancy of colour and intricate design of the original manuscript. There is also a facsimile copy of the Gospels.

In AD 793, the Anglo Saxon chronicle mentions 'sheets of light rushing through the air and whirlwinds, and fiery, dragons flying across the firmament' in Northumbria and this was said to be followed by a great famine. In the midst of these natural disasters, the first Viking raid in Britain took place on the Monastery of Lindisfarne on Holy Island by pirates from Scandinavia in search of wealth, slaves and new lands to settle. The Legacy of the Vikings film and exhibition in the Lindisfarne Centre gives you an insight into these dreadful times.

To help maintain the Centre and other facilities and services you will be asked to pay a fee to enter the exhibition area. On the other side of the road is the Gospel Garden and just up from there on the right is the Post Office. If you walk to the end of the road and look to your right, you will see the village school. When the tides are favourable, the children attend school at Lowick on the mainland, but when the causeway is closed the school on the island is used.

The Lindisfarne Centre is open all year and can be contacted on 01289 389004.

The Lindisfarne Gospels

In the seventh and eighth centuries the monastery on the island was regarded as one of the finest centre of religious learning and craftsmanship in Europe. This was exemplified by the creation of the Lindisfarne Gospels between AD 715 and AD 720 in honour of St. Cuthbert. These are now recognised as one of the world's greatest pieces of art. They are believed to have been written and painted by just one man, Bishop Eadfrith of Lindisfarne.

The Lindisfarne Gospels also contain the oldest surviving translation of the Gospels into the English language as around AD 950 - 960 one of the monks, Aldred added his Old English translation between the lines of Latin.

Made from more than 250 leaves of high-quality vellum, the manuscript holds the texts of the four Gospels in Latin, with appropriate introductory material, including a set of Canon Tables.

Tiny drops of red lead were used to form backgrounds, outlines or patterns, the initial page of St. Luke's Gospel has over 10,000 dots. There are five carpet pages, a page for each Evangelist, as well as large initial pages for the beginning of each Gospel. The original leather binding had an outer covering of gold with silver and gemstones added in about the middle of the eighth century.

The original Lindisfarne Gospels are in the British Library in London. There are facsimile copies in a glass case in St. Mary's Church on the island and in the Lindisfarne Centre, where there is also an interactive display.

The Lindisfarne Gospels. The Incipit page of St. Luke's Gospel opens with decorated script giving the opening words (incipits). Note the cat who has devoured a procession of birds. The cat sometimes symbolised evil and was the Celtic equivalent of Cerberus, guardian to the entrance of the underworld

The Lindisfarne Gospels. St Matthew's Gospel carpet page. This ornamental page stands opposite the beginning of St. Matthew's Gospel

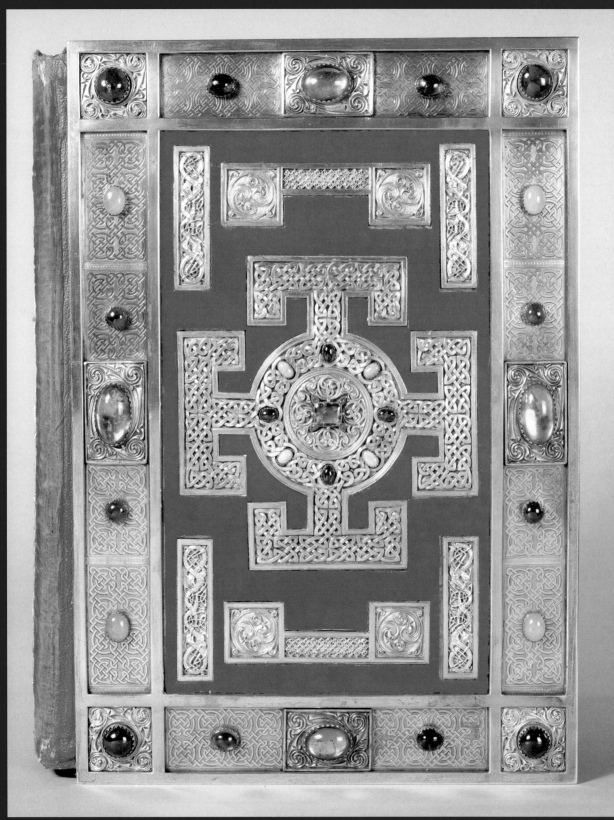

The upper cover of the 1853 treasure binding of the Lindisfarne Gospels, commissioned by Bishop Maltby of Durham and based upon the volume's carpet pages

The Harbour

The harbour has the famous upturned boats that are now used to house fishing gear by the island's fishermen. They are the remains of the island's nineteenth century herring fishing fleet that in its heyday was very important. Most of the herring were cured for export to the Baltic countries and a red brick curing house still stands on the green above the harbour. Another is found in the long building behind the last house on your left as you walk down the main street towards the castle. This last house was once a pub called the Iron Rails and was one of the nine that served the island in its fishing and industrial heyday.

Look to the west and you will notice that a steep drop curving around to the north borders the field in front of the Priory with a footpath running across it. This is the original harbour wall of the sixteenth century and shows the size of what was a strategically important naval base. Do bring your camera with you as there some amazing photographic opportunities amongst the lobster pots, ropes, floats and pallets.

The name for the harbour is the Ouse and a walk around it can offer you an interesting hour. It was protected by the stone fort known as Fort Osborne, built in the early eighteenth century that stands on the eastern end of the Heugh. Look through the gun ports and you will get much the same view as its early occupiers.

Access to the harbour from the sea is gained by the two navigation pillars you can see on the south shore. The Dundee Company which built the limekilns and jetty below the castle built them. Craft approaching line up both pinnacles so it appears that only one can be seen and they then know they are in the deep-water channel. The east navigation beacon is approximately 23 metres high whilst the western one is about 25 metres high. The original wooden pillars are still inside the nineteenth century outer sandstone ashlar

shell and these two tall, very slender, tapering pyramids, about 150 metres apart, were built some-time between 1820 and 1840 for Trinity House by John Dobson.

The Heugh

The Heugh forms the southern wall of the harbour and is a vantage point from which to view the interior of the Priory and the original harbour wall, now some one hundred meters inland. You also get stunning views of Lindisfarne Bay, Bamburgh Castle and the Farne Islands.

An information board that gives an excellent explanation of all the buildings here is sited just as you climb onto the Heugh from the walk across the meadow. At the eastern end of the Heugh, you will find the remains of a small fort built in the 1670s to protect the harbour. Further to the west are the war memorial and the old coastguard lookout tower now used as a bird observatory. Beside the tower is what's left of another small fort, whilst beneath it on the beach is the site of the original lifeboat station where you can still see the remains of the slipway at low tide. The Heugh also gives an excellent view of St. Cuthbert's Island.

Above and left: Scenes around the Harbour

Lindisfarne Castle

Perched on top of a mound of volcanic rock known as Beblowe Craig, Lindisfarne Castle can be seen for miles around. Constructed of stone taken from the Priory and built around 1550 the castle was intended to protect the harbour, at that time an extremely strategic and important port, from raids by the Scots. We know, for example, that in 1543, an army was based on the island and ten warships were at anchor in the harbour.

As you walk up the ramp to the castle entrance, you will notice three upturned herring boats now used for storage, similar to those down by the harbour. They are the remains of a Norwegian vessel called the 'Lorgresund' which was used during the Second World War on the famous 'Shetland Bus' escape route across the North Sea and at the same time took agents and supplies to Norwegian resistance fighters. She was brought down to Lindisfarne, sawn into three sections and the bow and stern placed here.

The castle did not see that much action in its time but during the Civil War suffered an unsuccessful six week siege by Royalist troops, who had captured Berwick.

However, in 1715 one Lancelot Errington and his nephew Mark managed to evict at gunpoint the two soldiers occupying the castle, hoist the Jacobite flag and wait for reinforcements. Unfortunately the only troops who arrived were loyalist soldiers from Berwick and the Erringtons were soon captured and interned in Berwick gaol, from which they almost immediately escaped by digging a tunnel. They hid in a pea-stack at Bamburgh for several days until they made their way to safety!

By 1820 the castle's use as a fort was over and its guns were removed. It became a coastguard station and for a while a base for the local militia and volunteers. This last role finished in 1885 and as a result the building was deserted and started to fall into considerable decay.

In 1902, the castle was bought by Edward Hudson, the owner of 'Country Life' magazine, who employed Sir Edwin Lutyens, one of the greatest architects of the day, to restore the derelict building. For the next nine years, work continued and resulted in the amazing conglomeration of styles and effects we see today.

Lindisfarne Castle

Hudson and Lutyens were both fascinated by seventeenth century Dutch interiors, so they commissioned photographs of the Lutyens's children at Lindisfarne in the style of Vermeer's paintings.

Charles Rennie Mackintosh, the Scottish architect, made a drawing of the castle when he visited Lindisfarne in July 1901.

Gertrude Jekyll tried to plant flowers on the sheer faces of the castle mound by lowering down a boy in a basket to do the job. Very few plants survived in the salt, wind and cold.

The walled garden designed by Gertrude Jekyll

The entrance to the castle no longer has its protective parapet, but the portcullis can still be seen as you pass through. To walk around the interior of the castle is an experience in itself, as rooms seem to change from a comfortable warm home to a stark late-medieval living and back again with a series of shapes and styles constantly emerging. Lutyens' genius was to construct the rooms and passages in such a manner that they seem almost to have been carved from the living rock.

The designer's genius can be seen in places such as the Ship Room's windows with what appear to be medieval stone seats, whereas both the windows and seats were inserted by Lutyens. These windows face north and overlook one of the gems of this property. Some five hundred meters from the castle lies a walled garden, designed in 1911 by Gertrude Jekyll and now restored, as far as possible, to her original plan by the National Trust. The plants have been chosen to match her detailed planting plan and although some are no longer available, enough have been sourced to recreate the splendour of the original garden, as it would have been in Hudson's time. He used the castle as a summer residence so the walled garden is planted to look its best at that time of the year. When the castle was used as a garrison it was probably a vegetable garden.

Gertrude Jekyll was born in 1843 and lived until she was 89 years old. She was an influential artist, gardener and craftswoman who designed over 400 gardens and wrote over 1,000 articles for Country Life, The Gardener and other publications. Hudson's architect, Sir Edwin Lutyens, and Gertrude were friends and she worked on garden plans for over 100 of his projects. Gertrude met Lutyens in 1889, when he was only twenty years old and they collaborated in the design for her new house and garden at Munstead Wood. She would supply the plants for her plans from her nursery garden and this is how she made her money as she never charged for her designs. Nowadays the seedlings for this garden are raised at Wallington, another National Trust property in Northumberland, and with its impressive Hall, walled garden, woodland and lakes, it is certainly worth a visit.

The Hudsons' guests were amongst the elite of the day and included the Prince and Princess of Wales, future King George V and Queen Mary, who complained that the cobbles hurt her feet. Lord Baden Powell, founder of the Boy Scouts, the ballerina Alicia Markova, J.M.Barrie, Herbert Asquith and the exotic Portuguese cellist, Madame Guilhermina Suggia were amongst the rich and famous who graced the castle.

Edward Hudson sold the castle to Oswald Falk, a London stockbroker, in 1921 for £25,000. After only a few years the castle was bought by Sir Edward de Stein, a successful merchant banker, pianist, watercolourist, and gardener. His sister Gladys was encouraged to use the castle as a family home for nephews and nieces during the holidays and he was happy to see it used by friends.

In 1944 Sir Edward de Stein, presented the property to the National Trust and so it became the Trust's first twentieth century house. Sir Edward remained as its tenant until he died in 1965 and his sister Gladys took over the tenancy until her death three years later. A stained-glass window commemorating the de Stein family is to be found in the church of St. Mary the Virgin.

In spring and summer the rock face plays host to stonecrop, viper's bugloss and other plants. The most notable wildlife you'll find here though is the fulmar. These birds nest on the ledges of the castle and are members of the albatross family. Although ungainly on land, fulmars are the most graceful and effortless of flyers.

Main Photo: Lindisfarne Castle / Inset: Fulmar

The Limekilns

Lime quarrying on the island started with the monks in the Middle Ages, but in the mid-nineteenth century, a Dundee company began to develop this activity on an industrial scale. Lime was produced by heating limestone in these kilns to 825 degrees centigrade to drive off the carbonic acid and moisture. Lime was extensively used in the building and chemical industries and was spread over farmland to improve crop yield.

This industry has left its mark on the island in the three distinct signs still visible on the landscape today: the remains of the wooden jetty below the castle where the lime was loaded to be shipped to Scotland can still be seen; the lime was quarried on the north of the island and brought down on a waggonway that is still used as a footpath to this day. The well preserved 19th century limekilns, just below the castle, are now in the care of the National Trust. The fiery glow from these limekilns, lighting the way for the horses and wagons to carry the lime to the jetty, can be clearly seen in the painting *The castle and Lindisfarne Abbey, Holy Island, by Moonlight* by John Moore now hanging in Lindisfarne Castle. Painted in 1877, it shows the castle before the restoration by Sir Edwin Lutyens.

There were also limekilns on the south-western area of the dunes, just about where the road comes onto the island and takes a sharp right turn before the car park, and a waggonway ran here too. The trade lasted some forty years before the five ships that plied between the island and Dundee stopped making the return journey loaded with coal for the kilns and taking away the lime.

However, the legacy can be seen on the southern shore opposite the castle in the form of the two obelisks that are still used by shipping today to find the safe channel into the harbour.

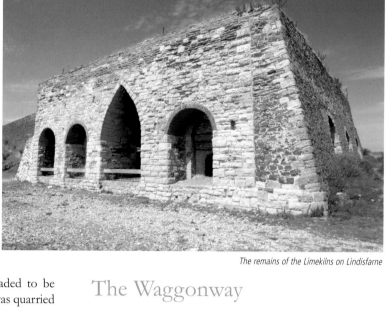
The remains of the Limekilns on Lindisfarne

The white triangle at Emmanuel Head

The Waggonway

The waggonway runs from the top of the limekilns to the north of the island and brought limestone to the kilns, a trade which at one time employed over 20% of the island's male population. Today it makes an excellent footpath to walk up to the quarries just to the south of Coves Bay. On the way you will pass the Lough, this is an interesting word in itself as it is the Celtic version of Loch as in Belfast and Strangford Lough and gives some possible clue to the age of this small lake. It may well have been used by the original monks for freshwater fish but today it acts as a bird reserve and you can see merlin here as well as several other species, and in the migration periods it can be veritable goldmine for the birdwatcher.

Merlin

The white triangle you can see as you near the north-east corner of the island, Emmanuel Head, is the day marker warning shipping about the dangerous reef in the middle of the bay. The next bay along has cliffs with caves at their feet.

There were other waggonways across the island and the route of one can still be seen at the west end near Chare Ends where there was a smaller complex of limekilns with workmen's cottages. The north of the island also has a small coal-seam and iron nodules were quarried here too.

Lindisfarne Castle

Local Information

Transport

The local bus service, number 477, operates to and from Berwick-upon-Tweed when the tides are favourable. For most of July and August this is a daily service but for the rest of the year it may be less frequent. For up-to-date information, contact the Berwick-upon-Tweed Tourist Information Centre on 01289 330733. Newcastle-to-Berwick buses on routes 505 and 515 stop on the A1 at Beal, which is 5 miles from Holy Island across the causeway.

A minibus shuttle service runs between the main car park, the Market Place and Lindisfarne Castle from Easter until the end of October depending on the tides and castle opening times. Check the island's website for information on taxis and buses: www.lindisfarne.org.uk

Shopping

On Lindisfarne the few shops are mostly found on Front Street and offer some beautiful examples of Celtic style gifts as well as books and clothing.
The Island Store, off the Market Place and the Post Office in Marygate are good places to buy books, souvenirs and basic holiday goods.
Celtic Crafts stocks a wide range of Celtic themed gifts including wedding rings and jewellery.
Sally's Cottage, next door to Celtic Crafts, has a good selection of gifts.
The Lindisfarne Scriptorium is the place for illuminated calligraphy and Celtic inspired artwork.
The National Trust shop has a wide variety of quality gifts and some particularly relevant to their property on the island, Lindisfarne Castle.
The Priory Museum shop has a wide range of gifts and books.
St Aidan's Winery make their own world famous Linidfarne Mead on the island and you are very welcome to a taste in the Winery Showroom. The monks at the Priory had their own brew house and may well have made mead. Honey was collected from hives at Beal (Bee Hill) on the mainland. As well as mead, St Aidan's Winery make speciality liqueurs and fudges and stock an extensive range of malt whiskeys, handcrafted beers and ciders along with speciality drinks and food. The Lindisfarne Craft shop specialises in stocking hand thrown and crafted Northumbrian Pottery, an extensive range of Celtic jewellery, Celtic throws, glass ware and pewter.

Food and Drink

The opening hours of many eateries on the island are dependent on favourable tides and the time of year so it is always best to check. There is a good choice of places for lunches and evening meals including The Crown and Anchor, The Manor House Hotel, The Ship and The BeanGoose Restaurant, next to the Lindisfarne Priory Museum. The Lindisfarne Hotel, the Island Oasis Café, Pilgrims Coffee House and The Stables Café are only open during the day. Some shops sell sandwiches and ice cream. There is a fantastic view of Lindisfarne Castle from the garden of The Manor House Hotel and this makes it a favourite refreshment stop for Catherine and her dog Ben. *(Photo by Sheila Hignett)*.

On the mainland, between Holy Island and the A1, there is The Barn at Beal with its café and restaurant. From the terrace there is a marvellous view of Holy Island with Bamburgh Castle in the distance. With a Birds of Prey Centre, walks and trails it is a good place to visit when you have to leave Holy Island early in the day due to the tide times.